Meet the Royals

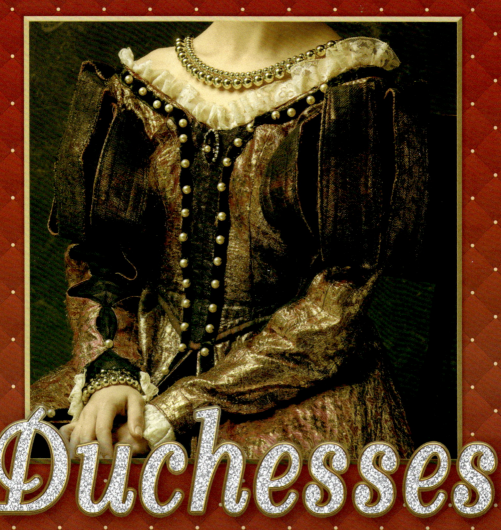

Duchesses

Enslow Publishing
101 W. 23rd Street
Suite 240
New York, NY 10011
USA

enslow.com

Sarita McDaniel

charity A group that helps people in need.

citizen A person who lives in a certain place.

duchy An area ruled by a duke or duchess.

monarchy A country that has a king or a queen.

related Part of the same family.

royal Someone who is a member of the monarchy.

symbol Something that stands for something else.

title A word or words used with a person's name to show an honor or rank.

Contents

Words to Know 2

Who Runs the Country? 5

The Royal Family 7

A Royal Wedding 9

Helping the King 11

Duchy Rule 13

A Princess and a Duchess 15

A Royal Duchess 17

Changing Roles 19

Modern Duchesses 21

A Symbol of the Crown 23

Learn More 24

Index 24

Britain's Queen Elizabeth II was crowned in 1947.

Who Runs the Country?

A place that is ruled by a king or queen is called a **monarchy**. The job of king or queen is usually passed from parent to child.

Fast Fact

Kings and queens rule about 40 countries around the world.

King James I of England and his wife, Queen Anne of Denmark, had children who were princes and princesses.

The Royal Family

Kings and queens may have brothers, sisters, and children. They are all part of the **royal** family. Each person in the royal family has a **title**. They may be princes, princesses, dukes, or duchesses.

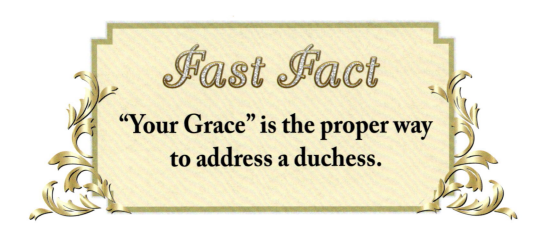

Fast Fact
"Your Grace" is the proper way to address a duchess.

When Britain's Prince Harry married Meghan Markle, they became the Duke and Duchess of Sussex.

A Royal Wedding

A duke may marry someone who is not royal. His wife becomes part of the royal family. Now she is a duchess.

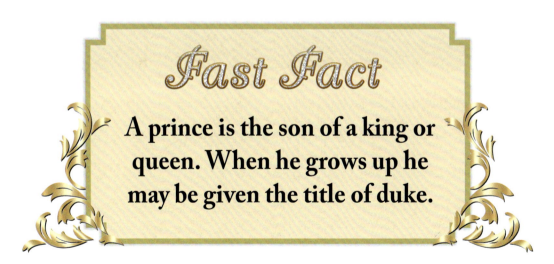

Fast Fact

A prince is the son of a king or queen. When he grows up he may be given the title of duke.

Many dukes and duchesses live in a castle or palace. This bedroom belonged to the Duchess of Aumale at Chantilly Castle in France.

Helping the King

Long ago, being a duchess was a big job. A duchess ruled over a **duchy**. This is a small part of a kingdom. Dukes and duchesses helped the king.

Fast Fact

Two *Harry Potter* films were shot at the castle of an English duchess.

Maria Teresa is the Grand Duchess of Luxembourg. Her husband is the Grand Duke.

Duchy Rule

Luxembourg is a duchy. It is the only one that is still ruled by a duke. Countries like England and Spain still have duchesses. But those duchesses do not rule over anyone.

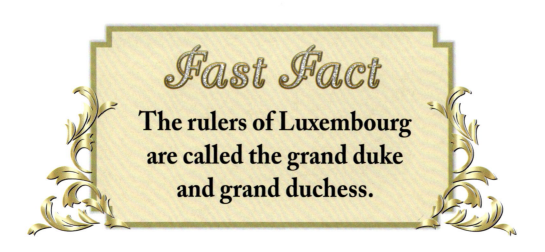

Fast Fact

The rulers of Luxembourg are called the grand duke and grand duchess.

A tiara is a kind of crown worn near the front of a woman's hair.

A Princess and a Duchess

Some duchesses are the daughters of kings and queens. They have two titles. They are princesses as well as duchesses.

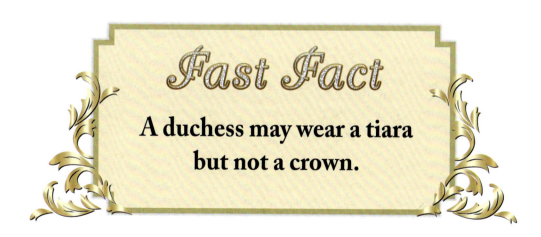

Fast Fact
A duchess may wear a tiara but not a crown.

Sweden's Crown Princess Victoria is also a duchess. She is the oldest child of the king of Sweden.

A Royal Duchess

A duchess who is **related** to the king or queen is a royal duchess. Duchess Victoria is from Sweden. She is also the Crown Princess. She will be a queen one day.

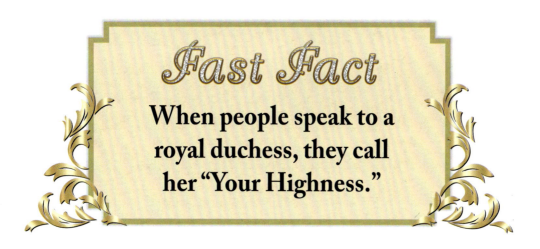

Fast Fact

When people speak to a royal duchess, they call her "Your Highness."

The Duchess of Cornwall appears at an event in Bath, England.

Changing Roles

Today, duchesses do not make choices for the country. They are a **symbol** of the royal family. They go to events around the country.

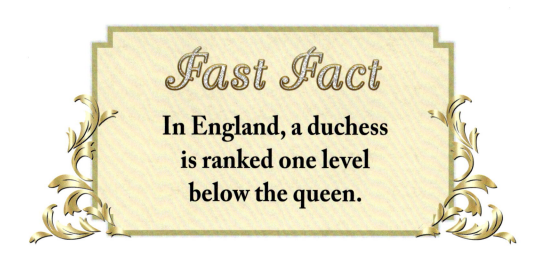

Fast Fact

In England, a duchess is ranked one level below the queen.

The Duke and Duchess of Sussex visit with children at a charity event.

Modern Duchesses

A modern duchess works with **charities**. She helps people in need. She works with groups to solve problems. She speaks to the **citizens** of the country.

Fast Fact

The Duchess of Sussex works with charities for the arts, education, animals, and women's rights.

The Duchess of Cambridge toasts the Chinese president at a state dinner.

A Symbol of the Crown

A duchess travels a lot. She talks to important people. She meets presidents and kings. Her visits help countries stay friendly.

Fast Fact

The Duchess of Cambridge will be Queen of England one day.

LEARN MORE

BOOKS

DK. *Castles*. New York, NY: DK, 2019.

Gagne, Tammy. *Meghan Markle*. Hallandale, FL: Mitchell Lane, 2019.

Zeiger, Jennifer. *Queen Elizabeth II*. Chicago, IL: Children's Press, 2015.

WEBSITES

DK Find Out! Kings and Queens
dkfindout.com/us/history/kings-and-queens/
Learn more about monarchs throughout history.

The Home of the Royal Family
royal.uk
Find out more about the British royal family.

INDEX

charity, 20, 21
duke, 7, 8, 9, 10, 11, 12, 13, 20
England, 6, 13, 18, 19, 23
king, 5, 6, 7, 9, 11, 15, 16, 17, 23
Luxembourg, 12, 13
prince, 6, 7, 8, 9
princess, 6, 7, 15, 16, 17
queen, 5, 9, 19, 23
royal duchess, 17
royal family, 7, 19
tiara, 14, 15

Published in 2020 by Enslow Publishing, LLC
101 W. 23rd Street, Suite 240, New York, NY 10011

Copyright © 2020 by Enslow Publishing, LLC

All rights reserved.

No part of this book may be reproduced by any means without the written permission of the publisher.

Library of Congress Cataloging-in-Publication Data

Names: McDaniel, Sarita, author.
Title: Duchesses / Sarita McDaniel.
Description: New York : Enslow Publishing, 2020. | Series: Meet the royals | Includes bibliographical references and index. | Audience: Grades K-3.
Identifiers: LCCN 2019008259| ISBN 9781978511996 (library bound) | ISBN 9781978511972 (pbk.) | ISBN 9781978511989 (6 pack)
Subjects: LCSH: Monarchy—Juvenile literature. | Kings and rulers—Juvenile literature.
Classification: LCC JC375 .S264 2020 | DDC 321/.6—dc23

LC record available at https://lccn.loc.gov/2019008259

Printed in the United States of America

To Our Readers: We have done our best to make sure all web addresses in this book were active and appropriate when we w to press. However, the author and the publisher have no con over and assume no liability for the material available on th websites or on any websites they may link to. Any comment suggestions can be sent by email to customerservice@enslow.c

Photo Credits: Cover, p. 1 Master1305/Shutterstock.com; PA Images/Getty Images; p. 6 Hulton Archive/Getty Ima pp. 8, 20 WPA Pool/Getty Images; p. 10 Micheline Pelle Decaux/Sygma/Getty Images; p. 12 Raymond Reuter/Syg Getty Images; p. 14 Tim Graham Photo Library/Getty Ima p. 16 Pascal Le Segretain/WireImage/Getty Images; p. 18 C Jackson/Getty Images; p. 22 Dominic Lipinski/AFP/G Images; cover, p. 1 (background), interior pages (borders) A Syplyak/Shutterstock.com, cover and interior pages (decora motifs) View Pixel/Shutterstock.com.

24